HERMANN BECK
Law and later San
sor of Oriental Stud
Berlin. A master of ancient and modern languages, he wrote extensively on religious and philosophical subjects, including Buddhism, Indology, Christianity, Alchemy and Music. In 1911, he heard a lecture by Rudolf Steiner and was inspired to join the Anthroposophical Society, where he soon became a valued co-worker. In 1922, he helped found The Christian Community, a movement for religious renewal. His many books are gradually being translated from the original German and published in English.

# HYMN TO THE EARTH

*From the Old Indian Atharvaveda*

With an Introduction and Commentary
by Hermann Beckh

Edited by Dr Katrin Binder and N.V.P. Franklin, Ph.D.

Translated by Maren & Alan Stott

TEMPLE LODGE

Temple Lodge Publishing Ltd.
Hillside House, The Square
Forest Row, RH18 5ES

www.templelodge.com

First English edition published by Temple Lodge in 2024

First German edition published under the title *Der Hymnus an die Erde, Aus dem altindischen Atharvaveda übersetzt und erläutert* by Verlag der Christengemeinschaft, Stuttgart, in 1934



A CIP catalogue record for this book is available from the British Library

ISBN 978 1 915776 20 4

Cover by Morgan Creative featuring 'Monhegan' by N. Roerich
Typeset by Symbiosys Technologies, Visakhapatnam, India
Printed and bound by 4Edge Ltd., Essex

# Contents

# A. Introduction

## 1
## *Age and origin of the* Hymn

In one of the oldest books of mankind, the Indian Atharvaveda, a *Hymn to the Earth* is found at the beginning of the twelfth section. It still speaks in a strong and lively voice to us today, or again today, through its poetic movement, the richness and beauty of its pictures, the profundity of its thoughts. All this charmingly paired with the naive vigour of the early people still living close to nature. This *Hymn* can be felt as a core document of primordial Aryan civilization. Although it originates far back in a pre-Christian age, it contains much that can be of significance in a Christian age.

Because of the uncertainty of all historical definition in Indology, the questions so essential and obvious to us today concerning the exact age of a poetic work can only be answered approximately. Of the four Indian Vedas[1]—Veda means knowledge, primordial wisdom—the *Rigveda* is usually regarded as the oldest book of Aryan humanity. Sanskrit researchers place it, or its 'oldest parts', as far back as the second millennium before Christ, whereas the later 'younger parts' reach back to the first millennium, even to the middle of it. Thereby it would go back to the time around Buddha (500 BCE), which is quite improbable, for the age of Buddha has the character of a late decadence; everything about the Vedas on the other hand has the character of great antiquity. For Buddha himself and the Buddhist writers the Vedic documents are of inconceivable antiquity, of a primordial time lost in the veil of the incalculable, for which at the present time we can find no standard or gauge. Consequently, we will have to concede to what is called the 'younger', or more recent part of the Veda a much higher age than the scholars want to admit.

Based on certain astronomical indications in the Veda—concerning the vernal equinox and the Pole Star—a renowned Sanskrit researcher (Prof. Jacobi in Bonn) wanted to ascribe to the Veda, to the Rigveda, initially an age one millennium earlier. Because a colleague contradicted this, he withdrew his hypothesis. Anthroposophy helps us to divine today the kernel of truth which it did possibly contain, by allowing us to recognize the connection of the great cultural epochs of humanity with the periods of the cosmic year and with this the realities of the—prehistoric—primordial Indian cultural age with its beginning reaching into the eighth millennium before Christ (vernal equinox in the sign of the Crab). At the same time, it is emphasized that no documents of any kind exist from this far-off primordial time, that also any Vedic tradition is only a later echo, yet one reaching back to the millennia of this ancient spiritual, primordial culture.

Although in this sense we speak of Vedic tradition, we should not initially think of written records. The oldest Indian manuscripts—written on birch bark—come from the post-Christian early Middle Ages. The Veda tradition was originally—through the centuries and millennia—a purely oral one, whereby we have to recall that the memory of people of those early times was incomparably more highly developed and more accurate than the memory today. One could even say that essential uncertainties and mistakes of a tradition only began to occur when it was put into writing.

Sanskrit researchers also admit that the Atharvaveda, along with the Rigveda, is particularly old. Winternitz in his

*Geschichte der indischen Literature* ['History of Indian literature'] (Leipzig 1908) believes he recognizes in the magic verses and hymns of the Atharvaveda an element reaching back into Indo-European primordial time. A certain similarity between medieval German forms of expression and such of the Atharvaveda has often been pointed out. Here one source has certainly not drawn from the other, so the conclusion makes sense that both reach back to a distant Indo-European primordial time. A similar relationship exists between the Rigveda song (X, 97) to the spiritual primordial human being (*purusha*) and that which in the Edda comes down to us as the primordial giant Ymir—some verses coinciding almost word for word suggest the common origin of both sources in Indo-European primordial time. We know that the recording of the Edda only took place during the Christian Middle Ages, so that some scholars doubt that it is older, whereas they recognize the Rigveda to be of an age at least reaching back some millennia.

With the Atharvaveda it is above all the magical content that makes it possible for the Sanskrit researcher to accept the early age. For the scholar it remains an open question whether this *Hymn* is extremely old, or to believe it belongs to the 'younger part' of this Veda. For the younger age of the Atharvaveda in comparison to the Rigveda the argument is that of the Indian predators in the Rigveda only the lion appears, whereas the tiger appears for the first time in the Atharvaveda. Only later when the Aryan peoples migrated from the north right down into the boggy lowlands of Bengal would they have got to know tigers (also mentioned in v. 49 of the *Hymn to the Earth*). But this whole reasoning is not conclusive. The emphasis of a 'different law' in v. 45, besides the differences of speech of the peoples, could rather be seen as something quite modern. But the

Indians themselves point back with their legal institutions to an unimaginably extreme age, right back to Manu, the founding father of post-Atlantean humanity.

Amongst the most charming aspects of the *Hymn* is that much in it that appears quite modern connects with what again points towards a distant prehistoric time. No doubt we are dealing here with a most precious piece of a most ancient poetic work of humanity, which we could quite modestly attempt to place at the end if not at the start of the second millennium before the beginning of our reckoning of time. Quite possibly, we could call this *Hymn to the Earth* the oldest modern poetical work, or the most modern piece of ancient poetry.

Its connection to the magical content of the Atharvaveda—in some verses this becomes clearly tangible—also speaks for the great age particularly of this *Hymn*. This 'magical element' belongs to the oldest times of the human past. Anthroposophy tells of the 'powers of nature' of ancient Atlantis—the reality of which is becoming today increasingly evident in the many realms of science. It speaks of the natural powers full of magic in the speech in that distant human primordial time (when the human being was still formed of a finer substance, more receptive to spiritual influence, of a more supersensible nature). It is natural that these magically powerful nature-forces of Atlantis penetrate especially into primordial Indian times as the earliest of the post-Atlantean cultures. But the Indian people are to fulfil other cultural tasks that lie more towards developing thinking. This increasingly estranges them from those powers of nature, increasingly internalizes their spirituality and increasingly estranges them from the Earth. We can call this later Indian spirituality that becomes increasingly inward *mystic*, the Indian—this can be shown right into the Indian path of knowledge, Yoga, which seemingly emphasizes the magical element—increasingly lays aside the magical element of primordial time and increasingly develops a mere mysticism. The Zarathustra-impulse, however, of primordial Iran[2] (that is, the primal Persian culture) strongly takes up once more the magical element of the primordial time and from there comes to its spirituality that strongly emphasizes work on the Earth, the fashioning and transformation of the earthly element.

The Indian is the primal mystic of humanity, the primal Persian, especially Zarathustra himself—the earlier Zarathustra mentioned by Plutarch, not the later one of the Avesta—is the primal magician. Precisely this statement, however, is not without meaning for understanding the Atharvaveda *Hymn to the Earth,* the Atharvaveda in general, also for any estimation of the time of its composition. It can make one wonder how the Indian 'estranged from the Earth', whose spirituality increasingly develops a one-sided mysticism, directs his gaze here towards a love for the Earth. With abundant devotion, with tender feeling, he speaks to Mother Earth, looks to nature with an intimate, artistic eye, giving himself to all the details. In contrast to the more abstract spirituality of other Vedic compositions, we can admire the poetic abundance of pictures, the colourful description in this *Hymn*. Here we can still feel something of the natural powers of primordial times. The Atharvaveda *Hymn to the Earth* is not influenced by the more mystical element of later Indian culture, but by the powerful magical element of nature from primordial times. The whole orientation of viewing the Earth corresponds to the magical spirituality turned towards the Earth and its fashioning. It inwardly follows logically that in the magical Veda, in the Atharvaveda, the Earth, and especially the

Earth, is celebrated as a spiritual being, as 'Mother Earth'. This expression 'Mother Earth', well-known to us, more Indo-European than Indian but also not strange to the Rigveda, can be found in several places within this Atharvaveda *Hymn*. This *Hymn*, like the Veda in general, has a more Indo-European, archetypal Aryan stamp than the soft character of later Indian culture as met—to mention the best example—in the poetry of Kālidāsa.

## 2
## *The name Atharvaveda; Indo-European and Indo-Iranian element of the poem*

Indeed, we can take a further step. When it was said that the Indian became estranged early on from the power of nature, from the magical element of the primordial time, whereas the Ancient Persian, the Iranian Zarathustra, was especially taken by this magical element once more, making it once more available to human development, then in the Atharvaveda, especially in the *Hymn to the Earth*, one could find, as it were, an Ancient Persian impact. This statement does not appear so far-fetched when we consider that *atharva* (*atharvan* the fire-priest, the oldest of all Indian words for 'priest') contains an ancient Persian expression in itself, that is a primordial Indo-Germanic word, which as such is contained in the Persian language, but—with the exception of this one compound word—otherwise is not contained in the Indian language. It is the word *athar*, 'fire', a Persian, not an Indian word, for 'fire' in Indian is *agni*, corresponding to Lat. *ignis*. This is already the earthly, sensory-visual fire. Contrasting to this the Persian word *athar* (which in Indian is only contained in *atharvan*,

Atharvaveda) appears related to the Gk. *aither*, is consequently the higher, not the physical but the 'etheric', the supersensible, the *magical fire*, out of which only later became the earthly flickering fire (*agni, ignis*) as a result of the 'Fall of man' (the 'Fall into matter') which coarsens everything earthly, bringing it into what is sensory and fixed. Teutonic mythology knows this historical fact of development as the 'chaining of Loki onto the rock' (of matter). Loki is the flickering flames of earthly fire.

We can consequently imagine that as already the name Atharvaveda contains an Ancient Persian element, the element of the magic primordial fire, that also in its content such primordial Persian-Iranian elements can be found. One may think of the glorification of fire in its different forms of appearance, which by gradually ever higher degrees appears in vv. 19-21 of the *Hymn to the Earth.*

Science today is increasingly aware of the fact how the human being carries the whole primordial past of his race and people in the complexes of his subconscious. These ideas, strongly materialistically coloured in today's world, receive their spiritual deepening and at the same time concrete explanation through anthroposophy, which shows how different peoples in different ways carry and preserve in themselves humanity's past. The Ancient Egyptians as well as the Hebrews, the Semitic people in general, carried much in themselves that belongs to the age in which the 'Fall' came to humanity, in which the power of death was increasingly felt, whereas in the Ancient Persian and Indo-Germanic peoples in the depths of their soul the memory lives of a still older primordial time. In anthroposophy this is called the 'Hyperborean age', the primal Paradise of humanity (whereas the later Paradise age described in the Bible, into which occurs the 'Fall', corresponds to the 'early Lemurian age'). Consequently, there lights up in the primordial Persian, in the primordial Indo-Germanic people, the Aryans in general, still a glimmer of the Hyperborean primordial fire, which was lost for later humanity through the consequences of the Fall. Consequently, there lives in Aryan people something which is essentially different from the pressure of sin of the Hebrew consciousness (one recalls the Psalms), which still allows him to lift his head in freedom towards heaven. Certainly, all possible consequences of the Fall already exist in the life of the Earth, humanity and animals—in the Atharvaveda *Hymn* this aspect of the description of earthly life is extensively present—but in the human being himself, in the Ancient Aryan, there always lives an element of primordial time that allows him to feel and enjoy the 'untouched freshness' of the Earth. A spark of the magical fire is still alive, which he knows relates to the 'secret fire' in the Earth's core and in the heights of heaven.

## 3
## *Content and structure of the* Hymn

It must have been somebody on the one hand deeply initiated into the primordial wisdom who received the inspiration of this *Hymn to the Earth*, or from whom it emerged; at the same time a poet who on the other hand knew how to adjust to the completely simple, naive manner of a primal people close to nature and to take them into consideration. The connection of this often childlike, naive element with the deep wisdom and sublime element calls forth the profound charm of this early poem. It still breathes the air of an existence close to nature, as the earliest Aryan Indians led their lives in the realm south of the Himalayas—which mountain range in the *Hymn* is beheld and celebrated with a splendid sense for nature. A breath of that which we today can still feel at times in certain foothills of the Alps weaves through this Atharvaveda *Hymn to the Earth.*

The translation offered here, which has been wrested from an extraordinarily difficult original text[3] in a long laborious work, without reference to any other existing translation that could have served as a reference or example, attempts with all endeavour to lay hold of the exact sense of the word, but at the same time to give the whole that poetic, artistic form that is demanded by the poetic movement of the original text.

Besides this poetic vitality of the poetic expression, we also become aware of the artistic structure, of the poetic meaningful and artistic build-up of the whole. A certain division into sections, possibly seven sections, seems to arise. An ever-recurring thought is that of the meaning of the activities of the priests, of the spiritual life in general, which proceeds from or comes through the human being for the development and the blessing of the Earth. The early Indian does not look at the Earth one-sidedly as something of material substance, but as a *spiritual being,* which takes part in everything that spiritually lives in the human being, which is held and carried by the spiritual life of the human being itself. Often, when this thought opening the whole *Hymn* re-occurs, this can be felt as the beginning of a new section: after an initial section where the Earth in its heights and depths, its fields and forests, seas and streams, with the majesty of its mountains, with everything that is carried within and without is celebrated, that recollection returns of the meaning of the activities of the priest in v. 13. The second section, which we could imagine begins here, culminates in the glorification of the fire that reigns in the Earth, on the Earth and above the Earth. Then in v. 22 the mention of the sacrifice and of making the sacrifice leads to a new section in which the motif of the *fragrance of the Earth* and its substances standing close to all cultic sacrifice is the essential thing. Less sharply pronounced is the transition to a further section, for example, with v. 26, which is introduced with certain formulas of veneration reminding us of the cultic ritual. Here, too (v. 29), it is once more mentioned how the Earth through the spiritual power of sacred prayer (*brahman*) receives forces of growth. In this section the motif of the balance holding up the earthly forces plays a main role and is gracefully developed in various ways. In v. 37 a further section is again clearly introduced with the activities of the priests—the Earth as the battlefield for gods and human beings appears here as the main motif. From here, an inner connection leads to the description of all the powers threatening earthly life in the animal world, in the human world and in the supersensory world. After this section has closed with a picturesque description of a thunderstorm there begins with v. 53 a seventh and final section in which looking up to the human being as lord of the Earth is the crowning conclusion. This verse expresses what the forces of the Earth and its elements also mean for the spiritual element of the human being. Here in this realm, we feel in particular closer to the Persian than the usual Indian culture. Here in vv. 60 & 61 the *Hymn* rises to the height of those wisdom-filled insights that we today connect with the name of Christ—for which in Indian culture there appears Vishvakarman—which are the wisdom-filled insights of the spiritual realities of the Earth, the penetration of the earthly element with the heavenly element.

In the Appendix more is mentioned of the shining through of these insights in the Atharvaveda *Hymn*. At first the *Hymn*, or rather the attempted translation, shall follow as text. Notes on this follow, providing explanations to the individual verses for further study. They also touch on more philological issues, important for friends and experts on ancient texts to check the translation.

In Sanskrit *ṛ* is spoken somewhat as in German *ri* (vowel r), y as Eng. *y*, v as Eng. *v*, c as *tsh*, j as *dsh*, ṭ, ḍ, ṇ with the tip of the tongue turned back, ś like *sh*, ṣ as *sh* with tongue turned back. Accents signify here the emphasized syllable; a line over the letter for long vowels, e and o are always long. In the translation Indian names are written in the accepted English manner.

## ATHARVAVEDA XII 1

1. *sátyaṃ bṛhád ṛtam úgraṃ dīkṣā tapó*
*bráhma yajñaḥ pṛthivīṃ dhārayánti*
*sā no bhūtásya bhavyásya pátny*
*uruṃ lókaṃ pṛthivī naḥ kṛṇotu*

...

8. *yārṇave 'dhi sálilaṃ agra āsīd*
*yām māyābhir anvacarán manīṣinaḥ*
*yasyā hṛdayaṃ paramé vyóman(t)*
*satyénāvṛtam ámṛtam pṛthívyāh*
*sā no bhūmis tviṣim balaṃ rāṣṭre dadhātu uttame*

...

11\. *gírāyas te párvatā himavánto*
*aráṇyaṃ te pṛthivi syónam astu*
*bábhruṃ kṛṣṇāṃ róhiṇīm viśvarūpāṃ*
*dhruvāṃ bhūmiṃ pṛthivīm indragúptām*
*ajīto ahato akṣato adhyaṣṭhāṃ pṛthivīm aham*

## B. *The Hymn to the Earth*
## (Atharvaveda XII, 1)

### *I*[4]

1. The great cosmic truth,
the sublime order of natural events and of religious life,
the priestly consecration and the conscientious inner work of the spiritual contemplative,
the sacred prayer and word, the sacrifice,
they maintain the Earth upright on its course.
This Earth, which for us governs everything that was and is still to come,
may it create a wide space for our existence,

2. and that we may be uncrowded by people [living] in their midst.
The Earth, to which belong the height and the sudden plummet, also the wide steppes,
the Earth, which carries the various strengths and virtue of the herbs,
may it stretch far for us and bless us.

3. On it is the ocean and the great stream,
on which the waters flow,
on which nourishment grows in the seeds of the field for the seeds of man,
the Earth, on which everything that breathes and moves has its being,
may it allow us to drink from its untouched freshness.
...

5. Upon it the early peoples of earlier times spread,
where gods fought against adverse demons,
and where the many kinds of cattle, horses and birds thrive,
the Earth, may it benevolently bestow on us happiness and splendour.

6. The one which carries everything and contains treasures,
which gives us firm ground, the secure support,
which carries gold in its breasts and is the home of all the world's beings,
which contains within the secret fire,
whose fructifying etheric force is the god Indra,
may the Earth place us in prosperity.

7. She, the Earth our homeland, above which gods are continuously watching without sleep,
may she give us the beloved honey,
indeed, may she shed her glory on us.

8. She, who at the primordial beginning of creation was the billowing primal waters,
upon whom, through their creative magic arts, wise seers were at work, traversing her,
she, whose heart, the Earth's undying heart, is in the highest heaven, enveloped by cosmic truth,
may she, our Earth, bestow on us glory and strength to make us the epitome of true rulers.

9. On whom the waters stream in the unchanging circulation day and night without end,
our Earth, may she bestow milk on us from many rays,
indeed, may she sprinkle us with her shining.

10. She, who once measured out the divine duality of the Morning Star,
who was traversed by Vishnu, the all-penetrating one,
who was once freed from enemies by Indra, the Lord of Strength,
may she, our Earth, stream her milk to me as does the mother to her son.

11. May the giants of your mountain-tops be for me protection and enjoyment,
your snow-covered mountains and forests, O Earth;
on the brown, black, reddish, many-coloured earthly ground,
on this firm Earth, well-protected by Indra,
on it will stand, unconquerable, unsurpassed, uninjured, on this Earth, I.

12. With that which is your centre, O Earth, that which is your navel,
and the nourishing juices that well from your body,
with this may we be blessed;
flow to us in streams, Mother Earth,
I am your son, the son of the Earth,
May Parjanya, the rain-god, her Father, bestow abundance on us.

*II*

13. On her the artists concerned with the consecrated sacrifice care for the consecrated altar,
and where they weave the mysterious threads of the sacrifice,
and where the sacrificial posts are set up, the pure ones before the pure offering,

she, this Earth, who herself grows and develops, may she help us for our growth.

14. The one who hates us, O Earth, the one who fights us with animosity,
who with the powers of thought or also with deadly weapons wants to do us harm,
give this one into our power, O Earth, be ahead of him.

15. Born from you we mortals walk upon you,
you carry two-legged humans and four-footed animals;
from you, O Earth, derive these five human races,
before whose mortality the immortal light in the sunrise spreads the fulness of its rays.

...

17. The one giving birth to everything, the mother of the plants,
the reliable, the constant Earth,
who is carried by the sacred world-order,
the well-meaning one, the benevolent,
let us always walk on her with gentle step.

18. You, who are our great homeland, your power is great,
mighty is your tempestuous jolt, your trembling, your earthquake;
may the great Indra unceasingly protect you.
O Earth, shine for us unceasingly in golden glory,
let nobody hate us.

19–20. Fire is in the Earth, fire in the plants,
the waters in the clouds carry fire in themselves,

fire is in the stones.
And thus there is inner fire in human beings,
fire is also in the cattle and horses;

the fire from heaven burns down from above
divine fire wafts in the wide space of the air;
on Earth this fire kindled by people,
is the god who carries aloft their sacrificial offering and is the friend of their sacrificial fat.

21. In her fiery dress, like a blacksmith with sooty knees,
may the Earth through the radiant fire temper me into a sharp polished edge.

*III*

22. On Earth mankind brings to the gods the correct ritual sacrifice
and from this once again mankind lives, the mortal ones,
also the offering to the manes, the nourishment for those who have died.
Of this may the Earth give us again strength to live and also long life,
may the Earth make a long life for me.

23. With this fragrance, O Earth, which arises from you,
which herbs and flowers carry in themselves and the watery sap,
which the beings of the air and of the water like to enjoy,
with this bestow fragrance on me, may nobody be our enemy.

24. With your scent, O Earth, as it penetrated the blue lotus-flower —

the scent-essence which for the first time at the wedding-feast of the Sun
was prepared by the gods, the immortal ones, in the primordial beginning—
with this bestow on me the scent, may nobody be our enemy.

25. With your fragrance, as it is in human beings,
in men and women, which seems lovely to us,
which is in horses and in the warriors on the horses, in wild gazelles and in elephants,
with this, too, which is the radiant blossoming of young girls, O Earth,
with this sprinkle us in blessing, may no-one be our enemy.

## *IV*

26. Rock is the Earth, stone and dust.
Thus is the Earth firmly put together.
To her, who carries gold in her breasts,
to the Earth I bring my veneration.

27. Upon whom the trees of the high forest firmly rooted stand for ever,
the all-nourishing, the all-retaining, the firm Earth we greet.

28. Whether we now get up or sit, stand or walk,
stride out with the right, with the left foot,
we do not wish to stumble on this Earth.

29. The purifying and pure one I greet, the patient Earth,
which through sacred prayer receives its increase.

On you, O Earth, who brings us the sap of life and nourishment,
the food that is right for us and butter, on you we want to build huts.

30. May your waters flow pure for our bodies;
may that which is impure belong to the adversary;
through purification by water I purify myself, O Earth.

31. Concerning the directions of the heavenly spaces, O Earth,
your East and your North, South and West,
may they all be mild and merciful to me wherever I walk;
do not let me fall, I who am thus firmly anchored in the universe.

32. Do not bring us out of our balance, O Earth,
do not push us forwards, backwards, upwards, downwards.
May you be for us salvation and well-being, O Earth;
may those waiting in ambush not find us,
keep from us the deadly bolt.

33. As long as with the Sun as companion
I may behold you, O Earth,
so long may the light of my eye not dwindle,
while I age from year to year.

34. When, lying on you I turn, O Earth,
from my right to my left side,
when, so that you turn your back to us,
we come to lie on you with our ribs,
then may you not hurt us, dear Earth,
you, who offer resistance to all.

35. May whatever I dig out of your lap,
quickly grow again, dear Earth;
I do not want, you pure one, to hit into the marrow of your life,
I do not want to bore through your heart.

36. Your summer, Earth, your rainy season,
your autumn, also your winter,
your spring and the cold time before spring,
all the seasons as they are well ordered upon you,
all the changes that occur from year to year, from day to night,
may they all quicken us.

## *V*

37–40. O you pure one, who drove away the snake,
on which the fires ignited which dwelt in the waters in the clouds,
with which you conquered the god-defying barbarian folk,
you who profess to Indra and not to the dragon,
you, Earth, who held to Indra, the bull-mighty Lord of Power.

Everywhere where the sacrificial room, the sacrificial roof, the sacrificial post is measured out,
where brahmins who know the sacrifice celebrate with sacrificial hymns and songs,
and where those trained to help in the sacrifice diligently prepare the soma-drink for Indra,
everywhere where the creative wise seer of primordial times
brought forth the kine of the light through song.

Within their sitting together as a group of seven
the holy Rishis through their sacrifice, through the power of their spiritual contemplation,
this Earth, may she always give us what we long for in riches,
may the Lord of Bread remain with us,
may Indra come to us, may he be our leader.

41. The Earth here on which the people sing and dance and jubilate in varied exuberance,
and where they fight, where the noise of the battle is heard, the drum calls for battle,
may this Earth expel our rival, may she free me from the adversary.

42. To the Earth, where our nourishment grows in rice and barley from the grains of the field,
where the fivefold seed of humanity cares for the seed of the field in a fivefold manner,
to the bride of the rain-god Parjanya, who becomes fat and fertile through the rain,
to her may veneration be brought.

43. On whom the divine strongholds of the highlands tower,
on whom in the lowlands the people struggle,
the Earth, which is the maternal lap of all,
may the Creator make it everywhere delightful for us.

44. What she bears as treasures in many places,
hidden goods, rock-crystals and gold,
may the Earth bestow on me as gifts.
The bestower of the good, may she bestow on us her goods,
the goddess Earth, the bestower of all, she of good-will.

45. The Earth, who bears such various peoples
of different languages, according to their homeland, and various laws, in various places,
may she bestow on me rich goods in a thousand streams,
like the faithful milch-cow who does not struggle.

## *VI*

46. Whatever snakes and scorpion-creatures with sharp bites and sting crawl away in winter,
and dully and rigidly lies hidden,
whatever then in the rainy season of the summer stirs,
comes forth and becomes alive, O Earth,
your crawling creatures, may they not creep on us;
may what is harmless and friendly meet us.

47. Where your many entwined ways exist,
on which people go, your roads,
where pleasure-carriages roll and heavy carts are driven,
where both good and bad people walk,
there we want to find our way,
which is free of enemies, free of robbers;
may what is harmless and friendly meet us.

48. The Earth, who carries the dumb idiot,
as well as the wise and sublime teacher,
she, who accepts the decline of the good as well as the bad with equanimity,
who is at peace with the wild pig, with the evil boar,
is also pleased to make room for the gazelle.

49. The wild animals of your forest, who wandering in the wilderness of the jungle,

there leading there their lives,
lions and tigers who attack people,
jackal and wolf, O Earth, and the were-wolf,
the demonic monster, shoo them far away from us.

50. The evil beings in the air and in the water,
nightmares and bad dreams,
all the devilish ghosts and demons,
hold them, Earth, far from us.

51–52. When in fear the winged beings of the air draw together,
wild geese, eagles, vultures and all the other fowl,
where then the storm, the wind's bride wildly sweeps along,
whirling up thick clouds of dust and bending the trees aside,
and where the rushing of the storm is followed by the bright flame,
where darkness and light follow each other in quick succession and unite,
which otherwise are separated as day and night on the Earth,
and where the Earth is completely saturated by rain,
then may she bring us affably into our dwelling, each one into his home.

## *VII*

53. The heaven and the Earth and the air,
they gave me the all-encompassing understanding,
the fire and the Sun and the water,
all the gods have gifted me with wise insight.

54. Indeed, I, the human being, I am he who can do anything,
I am the Lord of the Earth, I am the super-strong one,
indeed, the all-powerful, the all-mighty in all realms.

55. When, radiating in the first dawn of the early world,
you, goddess highly praised by the gods, poured out your splendour,
then a feeling of well-being penetrated you,
with this you filled all four directions of heaven.

56. In all the villages and in all the forests,
in places everywhere where people come together,
where they have their meetings, their assemblies,
there, Earth, we will proclaim your praise.

57. In the same way as a horse shakes off the dust,
thus she shook off the human races,
who from the beginning of their existence inhabited her:
as a lovely protectress of world she always went before,
she, the protectress of the trees, herbs and flowers.

...

59. Gentle, richly fragrant and mild,
carrying the sweet drink in her udder,
abounding in sweet milk,
thus shall the Earth offer me her drink with comforting words.

60–61. The one who was once sought by the divine-creative cosmic artist with his sacrifice,
when she kept herself hidden in the billows of the water and the air,

which then was revealed and became the enjoyment for
everyone born of a mother—
a precious chalice, closed and hidden,
you are the chalice, the heavenly Mother of Human Beings,
you are widely famed as the one who grants wishes,
that in which you lack is supplied by the cosmic Creator,
the Firstborn of the lofty cosmic order.

62. Thus may we, as the children of your lap,
be without illness, never exhausted, O Earth;
we strive to blossom towards our long life,
thus we will pay back the thanks we owe to you.

63. O Mother Earth, allow me in your gracious favour
always to be well grounded.
In agreement with the high heavens,
help me, you wise seeress, towards healing and happiness.

# C. Explanations to the *Hymn* and the translation

(The numbers refer to the verses of the *Hymn*)

For the spiritual powers that carry the life of the Earth the Indian language employs short words, for which, since modern languages do not possess the relevant concepts, translation sometimes has to look for longer paraphrases.

1. *satyam bṛhat* 'the great truth', the cosmic truth seen as a spiritually active power and being could still be shortly and simply expressed. Then there follows *ṛtam ugram*, the 'sublime *ṛta*'. For this word there exists no exact equivalent in German or any other language. The word derives from the root *ṛ* (a rolling *r* that is counted as a vowel, to be spoken vibrantly) 'to walk, to move oneself', which especially expresses rhythmic movement and is connected with the Gk. *rheo, rhein* 'to flow' (related to this, the name of the River 'Rhein' [Eng. Rhine], from which again there derives *rhythmos* 'rhythm'. One can consequently understand the Indian *ṛta* as the great order of the world, the cosmic order and the order of natural events as they are revealed in the laws of the stellar courses, in the rhythmic change of the seasons, that cosmic order which again is mirrored, reflected in the order of religious ritual. The word *ṛta* thus also means the order of the sacramental rituals, the rituals of sacrificial offering. Natural laws and religious order still coincide for Indians.

As a third related ordering power there follows *dīkṣa*, the priestly consecration, the initiation, the ritual of which is precisely described in the Brahmana texts. Through the consecration the brahmin [priest] enters the spiritual world, he is removed from the human into a divine sphere.

Then there follows in the fourth place a concept, which is in a special way suitable for the Indian spiritual life: *tapas* for which there is nothing that corresponds in modern languages. Asceticism practised in India since ancient times, often intensified to a self-torture, is called *tapas* in Sanskrit. This increasingly merges into the spiritual exercise of concentration, meditation, contemplation (for which there exists in Indian other words, such as *dhyāna*, *samādhi* etc.). The root of the word is *tap* 'to warm, to heat'. We also find this in Latin *tepidus* 'warm', or in the name of the watering place *Teplitz* ('warm springs'). The Indian knows spiritual exercising as a drawing together of warmth forces. In the Song of the Creation of the World of the Indian Rigveda (X, 1-9)—see translation in the Appendix—*tapas* appears as the creative musing of the primordial spirit igniting cosmic warmth, 'of the spiritual deepening power which brooding awakens world-warmth'. The account of creation of Manu uses in the same sense the word *dhyāna* 'meditation'. For the Indian *tapas* is consequently a world-creating and thus also a power continuing to carry spiritually the life of the Earth, not such as only serves the needs of the one practising. The Indian knows that all true spiritual effort ('effort' is at the same time the literal translation of the Indian word *yoga*) means something not only for the individual but also for the Earth and humanity.

That which was then expressed further in the translation with 'the sacred prayer and word', reads in Sanskrit *brahma* (root form *brahman* (the *h* to be spoken somewhat audibly) the central concept of Indian spiritual life, for which again there exists no exact or even approximate correspondence in modern languages. The word *brahman*, from the root *bṛh*, which is also presumed to lie at the root of the German *'Berg, bergen, verbergen'* (mountain, to protect, to hide), points on the one hand towards the great expanse, on the other hand to what is hidden, the Cosmic, or World Mystery. For the Indian it is initially the power connected to the sacred word, developed in prayer, in devotion, in meditation, which is felt as a mystic, hidden secret (occult) power. From this more subjective meaning, the word arrives at the object meaning of the *divine hidden in the world*, of the power which mysteriously weaves and works throughout the cosmos: the eternal *brahman*, the divine, cosmic word. The priest, the brahmin, is for the Indian particularly, the carrier of the *brahman*, of the mysterious, divine power, in a certain sense also the 'servant of the word'. In the Atharvaveda, in the first verse of our *Hymn*, we initially find the word used in its subjective meaning (the power of devotion, of prayer, of the sacred word), but in such a way that we can understand from this passage how it has arrived at its objective meaning as a power 'carrying and ordering' the life of the Earth.

In the Atharvaveda, in the fifth verse, to the spiritual powers carrying the earthly life there still belongs the sacrifice (*yajña*). In the sacred writings of the Indians, especially in the Brahmana texts we find repeatedly expressed that all world-becoming is begun through the creative sacrifice of the gods and is carried further through human sacrificial deeds. This thought forms the background to the whole Indian ritual, the whole Indian worship, the whole religious life of India. Already in everyday life we recognize how this life is kept going through lower beings giving themselves to those who are more highly developed, offering themselves as nourishment. (Many German readers know

Christian Morgenstern's beautiful poem *'Fußwaschung'*, 'The Washing of the Feet'.) Everything decisive, all progress in the events of the world, arises through sacrifice. The sacrifice in the ritual is an enacted mirror of this.

That the Earth is called the 'governess of everything that has become, and which is becoming' reminds one of the Egyptian saying of Isis, 'I am everything that was, that is and that shall be'. The bestowing of a wide space lies already in the word *pṛthivī* 'Earth', which is related to the German word *'breit'* ('wide') (Skt. *pṛthu*).

2. Instead of *badhyato* of the edition by Roth-Whitney, we read *madhyato* ('in the midst').

3. See in the Appendix for details on the connection to Christ with the word *kṛṣṭi*, which can be found in this verse, also vv. 4 and 42 and means 'ploughed field, a sown field', also 'human roots, human seed'.

'The Earth allows us to drink of its untouched freshness' (*no bhūmiḥ pūrvapeye dadhātu*) literally 'may she admit us to the first drink (from her beaker or chalice)'.

4. The fourth verse, omitted in the translation, appears like a weaker repetition of what has been said before and appears like a later addition of a lesser poet. Its translation would be: 'To whom the four directions of heaven belong, the Earth, where in the fields grows nourishment for human beings, the one who carries in many forms that which breathes and moves, she might help us to gain cows and everything else (richness).'

5. [No Notes]

6. The gold within the Earth ('in the breasts of the Earth') is often mentioned in the *Hymn*. We may recall Nietzsche's saying, 'the heart of the Earth is of gold' [*Thus Spoke Zarathustra*, 40, Great Events], especially regarding what is said in v. 8 of the 'heart of the Earth'.

The 'hidden fire', Indian *vaiśvānara* (emphasis on the third syllable from the end). The Indians everywhere distinguish the outer fire from the inner fire of the human being, *agnir vaiśvānara* (the 'completely human fire') to which many hymns of the Rigveda are dedicated. Rudolf Steiner points out how the fire is that phenomenon in the world that forms the bridge from the outside towards inside and from the inside out. Consequently, for the Indians *Agni* is the mediator from the gods to human beings, the connection between the sensory and the supersensory world—'whose fructifying ether-force is the god Indra', lit. 'for whom Indra is the bull'. Indra, the Indian national god, plays a significant role in the *Hymn to the Earth*. As the other Vedic divinities belong to other elements, Indra is assigned to the element of ether, as the 'fifth element', which the Indians still recognize besides fire, air, water and earth, and is assigned to the sense of hearing, the sense for sound (in the same way as fire and light belong to the sense of sight, air to the sense of touch and water to the sense of taste, and earth to the scent, to the sense of smell). As lord of the ether element, Indra also governs the ruling power of thinking. A hymn of the Rigveda (II, 12) speaks about how Indra, just born, was gifted with this power of thinking. As lord in the ether, Indra is also the god of thunderstorms, who wields the weapon of lightning, with which he combats the enemy dragon, the adversary threatening earthly life and earthly development. Consequently, Indra gains significance as the protector of the Earth, especially in this *Hymn to the Earth*.

7. Honey, as the embodiment of the most noble juices of nourishment, plays a role in Indian mysticism (for example, in the Upanishads).

8. Like the creation myth of the Bible, the Indian creation account also speaks of the etheric primordial

condition of the Earth as the 'billowing primordial waters'. The Indian seer describes the Earth not only as it presents itself at the present time to the sensory eye, but as it is seen by the spiritual eye in its whole metamorphosis of development. Famous in this regard is (see Appendix 1) the Creation Hymn of the Rigveda (X, 129). The *Hymn to the Earth* repeatedly returns to the events of the creation.

The early Indians recognize the forces of vision of the ancient seers (rishis) at the same time as active magical forces, through which they themselves creatively participate in fashioning the earthly element. The early Indians see the spiritually awakened human being participating in the work of creation.

The word of the divine-immortal 'heart of the Earth in the highest heaven' belongs to the most important places in the whole *Hymn*, belonging to its actual Mystery-depths. In the Appendix can be found more about the connections shining and sounding through here of Earth and Sun, Sun and starry world, and on the other hand, of Sun and heart, Sun and gold, gold and Earth. In the same way, concerning the connection of the heart with the 'cosmic truth' (*satya*), which reminds us of certain Egyptian motifs.

The realm of power (*rāṣṭra*, actually kingdom) of which the *Hymn* speaks is not an outer but a spiritual power; instead of 'to the highest (true) embodiment of the realm of power' we can thus also translate: 'to the highest ruling power in the "I"', all more reason, since—cf. especially v. 11—the 'I' in this *Hymn* is surprisingly strongly emphasized by Indian standards. Also, in the well-known expression *rāja-yoga* ('royal yoga') the 'kingdom' relates to the development of the 'I' as the actual aim of this highest form of the Indian meditative path of knowledge.

9. [No Notes]

10. The Indian name of the divine couple meant here is *Aśvin* (spoken Ashvin), *Aśvinau* 'the Ashvin twins'. They correspond, as the 'divine twins' to the Greek Dioskuri (Castor and Pollux). Their planetary aspect is connected by Oldenberg (*Religion des Veda*, p. 210ff.) with Venus, with her double appearance as the Morning Star and Evening Star; yet the Ashvin were always venerated as the divinity of the Morning. Perhaps one should rather think of Venus-Mercury, which in ancient times one had seen within a certain spiritual connection.

Vishnu (*Viśnu*), from a root *viś* (spoken vish) 'to penetrate' is the 'Son God' of the Indian trinity. Indian mythology speaks of 'the three steps' with which he strode through the earthly world in order to lift himself with the third step into a world of the highest light.

*Śacī* (*c* spoken like tsh), the 'spouse of Indra', is the essence of the higher ether force.

11. The 'snow covered mountains' (*parvatā himavanto* for the Indians are the tops of the Himalaya (Himavant), the highest mountains of the Earth. Beside *parvatā* stands here intensifying the word with the same meaning *girayaḥ* (plural of *giri* 'mountain'), rendered here as 'giants of the mountain tops' (one may also pay attention to the sounds in *giri*) which used in relation to the Himalaya is no exaggeration.

Regarding *kṛṣṇa* (spoken approx. krishna) 'black' see Appendix, which mentions its derivation from *kṛṣ* 'pull through, 'to furrow' (the black colour of the earth loosened up by the plough) and with a certain pre-linguistic connection of the name [strictly speaking a title] 'Christ' (as also the name of the Indian saviour *Kṛṣṇa*, Krishna).

12. Parjanya, the rain god (spoken pardshanya), is called in Lithuanian Perkunas. With such examples one recognizes the kinship of the Indo-Aryan languages.

13. In a characteristic way the *Hymn* emphasizes the significance of the cultic consecrated offering for the Earth's development. As common as this expression is for us today, it is most surprising in the Indian context. Except for one place in the Yoga Sutras (IV, 5) no other passage in the whole of Indian literature exists where this expression resounds so clearly. The Indian word is *vardhate* (3rd person singular) 'to become, to grow, to develop', causative verb *vardhayati* 'to bring into becoming, into growth, into development'. Both forms can be found in this passage of the Indian *Hymn*. The expression translated here with '*des Weiheopfers vielgeschäftige Künstler*', 'the artist most engaged with the consecrated offering', contains in the Indian the word '*viśvakarmānas*', pl. of *viśvakarman* (spoken vishvakarman), which, according to Rudolf Steiner, is the Indian Vedic name of the Christ-being (as it were, 'the creative world-artist', the '*Weltbaumeister*', 'Master-builder/ Architect of the World'; more concerning this in the Appendix). In this sense we also find this name in our *Hymn* verse 60, dedicated to the cosmic Mystery of the chalice of the Earth. It can appear significant, that right into the wording in a verse that points towards the spiritual significance of the priestly working for the Earth, those connections sound into it which connect us today with the name of Christ and its Mysteries.

14. [No Notes]

15. The 'five human races', according to the conventional explanation (Böhtlingk in the *Petersburger Wörterbuch*), are the tribes in the north, east, south, west, with the Aryans in the middle. The Indian word is here *pañca mānavāḥ*, derived from Manu (the name of the patriarch and leader of the first humanity), this name again from the root *man* 'thinking', which is also contained in the

Germ. *'Mensch'*, Eng. man (Indian *manuṣya*). At different places (vv. 3, 4, 42) we find here the word *kṛṣṭi*, about this more in the Appendix.

16. The meaning of this insignificant and most likely non-genuine verse, omitted in the translation, would be: 'Allow these creatures to give to us all kinds of fruit; bestow on me, O Earth, the honey of speech.'

17. *dharmanā dhṛtām* 'which is carried by the sacred ordering of the world': the Indian word *dharma* or *dharman* (related to the Lat. *firmus* 'firm') connects the concept of the natural law with the moral law in a way foreign to modern thinking.

18. It appears remarkable how especially here in connection with earthquakes and earth catastrophes Indra (as the 'conqueror of the dragon', the Indian equivalent of the Assyrian Marduk, of the Hebrew-Christian Michael) is described as the guardian of earthly life.

The connection of the uncanny powers of the interior of the Earth, of the 'core of the Earth', with the destructive, obliterating powers of hate with the human being, is a motif we also meet in Dante's *Divina Comedia* as the 'Cain chasm' or 'Cain layer' [*Inferno* 32].

19-20. About the 'inner fire' in the human being (*agnir vaiśvānara*), see the explanation of v. 6. Agni, the god of fire, appears clearly here in his role, known from the Rigveda, as the mediator between the gods and human beings in the ritual sacrifice.

21. The verse is also in Indian of a compressed, 'dashing' brevity: garment of fire and blackened ('sooted') knee clearly frame the picture of the blacksmith, although the word 'smith' does not directly appear in the Indian. With a light touch of the Upper Bavarian dialect, one could translate, *'Mir scharfen Schliff und Schneid' verleih'n'* [something

like 'to knock me into shape'], which would thoroughly correspond with the Indian original.

22. There begins a new section again with the indication of the importance of the ritual sacrifice for the Earth and humanity. Especially significant is the indication of the effect of the sacrifice also for those who have died, for the spiritual connection this establishes between the living and those who have died, and which streams back as a blessing effect extending the life of the living.

23. In connection with the meaning of the gift of offering, there is now also poetically expressed the motif of the *savour of the earth*, of the element of scent—one may think of the fragrance that streams from the earth after a thunderstorm, with that connection of naivety and sublimity typical of the *Hymn*. In the ordering of the 'five elements'—besides the four elements known to us, the Indians acknowledge a fifth, the *ether* (*ākāśa*, spoken akasha with a long 'a' for the first and second syllable)—for the senses and sense impressions the Indian always connects the earth with smell and the sense of smell, in the same way as water with taste; the air with touch, the sense of touch; fire and light with the sense of sight. The 'fifth element', ether, corresponds to sound, the sense of hearing.

For the anthroposophical path of knowledge, the element of earth is spiritualized in the life-ether, the water element in the chemical ether that is also the sound-ether, the element of air in the light-ether. The fire-element corresponds to the warmth-ether. The life-ether—belonging to the earth—seems to correspond with the element of scent in a similar way as the chemical ether—belonging to the water—corresponds with the sound-ether. Anthroposophy also teaches that scents serve certain elemental beings as nourishment, as a delight. Concerning this, *Occult / Esoteric Science* also speaks [Ancient Saturn evolution]; in the primordial development of the Earth, the fine substance of the 'element of earth' was like a scent essence, as we perceive through our organ of smell. With this we approach the content of v. 24.

24. It is remarkable how in this verse the divinity of the Sun (*sūryā*) still appears feminine, whereas in later Indian the word for 'Sun' (*sūrya*) is masculine. This corresponds to a connection in the development of the human 'I'-consciousness indicated in anthroposophy. The male [patriarchal] aspect, born out of the 'I', appears at a certain period taking the place of the feminine [matriarchal] aspect.

25. Here the 'naive' comes especially to the fore. The scent of the elephant oestrus also plays a role in Indian love poetry.

26. The unequal extension of the verses, its changing measure, as it were, its changing syllables contribute to the beauty of the *Hymn* and its composition. An attempt was made to reproduce this approximately in the translation, yet because of the difference of the German and the Indian language it was not possible completely to adjust the number of syllables to the original text.

27. In the Indian *viśvadhāyas* the concept of the all-nourishing as well as the all-preserving element is contained.

*vānaspatyās*—said about the trees in the forest—means literally 'the lords of the forest'.

28. *brahmaṇā vāvṛdhānām* 'which grows through holy prayer', through the more intensive form of the root *vṛdh, vardhate* 'become, grow, develop', expresses more strongly the notion of development. As already at the beginning, *brahman* appears here, the hidden (occult) strength of prayer, of the word, of devotion and meditation, as something belonging to the maintenance and shaping of earthly activity and participation and thus later becoming the

designation of the divine substance and essence in the universe in general.

29. [No Notes]

30. Literally 'what is unclean in ourselves, we dump on those who are not dear to us'.

31. [No Notes]

32. [No Notes]

33. In the noble thoughts of this especially expressive verse the epistemological connection vividly emerges between the Sun, vision, sensing/ meaning and being (earthly sense and earthly being).

34. [No Notes]

35. The strongly resounding 'naivety' in verse 34, in the counter-verse 35 experiences a delightful reversal, reminiscent of the soul-filled old Christmas plays [for example, from Oberufer, in Upper Austrian dialect], (*'grüaßen wir alle Würzelein, die unten in der Erde sein'*, 'let us greet all the little roots who are down in the ground').

36. The early Indian reckoned with six seasons; 'the rainy season' follows the summer, which follows spring (*vasanta*), preceded by the cold early spring (*śiśira*, spoken shishira, emphasis on the first syllable).

37–40. The *Hymn* brings us back to cosmogonic mythology, in which the battles of Indra with the enemy dragon (in addition to the main adversary Vṛtra, other dragon demons are also mentioned) plays a leading role. *Indraṃ vṛṇānā pṛthivī na vṛtram* 'you who acknowledges you belong to Indra, not the dragon': the Indian *vṛ* (here participle form *vṛṇānā*) according to its meaning as well as its sounds does not exactly correspond to our word 'choose'. In the sense of the myth there takes place, as it were, a cosmic act of voting, in which the Earth is to decide whether it chooses the divine leader, or the adversary, the enemy dragon, and the Earth chooses Indra. The meaning of the verse—consequently we too will stay with Indra-Michael as the true leader, the true Lord of the Earth.

At the beginning of v. 37, 'O pure one' (the Earth is meant), 'who chased away the snake' is especially to be compared with the Michael-chapter of the Apocalypse / Rev. (12:13ff.). The section also strongly reminds one of the Egyptian myth that recounts how Isis, chased by Typhon-Seth, flees with her child into the desert (the 'oasis cow-land') and there protects herself from the attacks of the adversary through taking on her earthly form of the cow[5]—especially Rev. 12:16: 'But the earth helped the woman by opening its mouth and swallowing the river that the dragon had spewed out of his mouth.' Here certain archetypal myths of humanity are involved, also mirrored in the Gk. legend of Io, in order to come to life again in a new form in the visions of the Christian Apocalypse.

The Mysteries of the soma drink and the soma preparation are closely connected to those of Indra. In the Rigveda, Indra is the divine reveller who enjoys the celestial soma drink. The earthly counter-picture and symbol of this celestial soma for the Indian is the milk-sap pressed out of the soma plant (*asclepias acida*), which the priests, the brahmins, enjoy mixed with milk during the soma sacrifice. Soma is the drink of enthusiasm, of the highest spiritual elevation, the symbol of eternal life, the 'cosmic provisions for the way' or the nourishment of the Grail. In the Rigveda (X, 85, 3) we read: 'Some who drink the soma believe it is pressed out of the herb; the soma, as known to the brahmins, no one enjoys in an earthly way.'

The Mysteries of Agni and of soma pervade the whole Rigveda. They contain the Indian, pre-Christian correspondence of the Christian Mystery of the Last Supper of bread and wine, body and blood.

41. The turning against the earthly adversary completely corresponds to the attitude in the ancient Aryan world. Only on the cross of Golgotha was the impulse to love one's enemy linked with the earthly [situation]. In the time hitherto, as Rudolf Steiner has often shown, anger, enmity and war had their mission in earthly development. What here is said of the outer adversary may be applied in a Christian age to the inner adversary.

42. Concerning the word *kṛṣṭi*, used here for the 'five human races', see the Appendix. Our rendering seeks to include both sides of the concept (seeded field and humanity). (Thus, already in v. 3.)

43. *puro devakṛtāḥ,* literally 'the god-created fortresses', which can only refer to the mountains. In this *Hymn* the natural feeling for the high mountains appears in an astonishing manner for this early age. So it is not right that, as is sometimes believed today, this attitude for the mountains was first discovered in the eighteenth or nineteenth centuries (for instance by Rousseau, *La nouvelle Héloïse*), for as we see the early Aryan Indians have already possessed it for millennia.

44. In Indian, *maṇi* signifies 'precious stone' and 'crystal', especially the mountain crystal, which is undoubtedly meant in the first instance.

45. [No Notes]

46. With this verse begins in a certain way the 'danger zone' of the whole work. Listed here are what the Earth produces of hostile beings in the animal world, the human world and the demonic world. Snakes, so dangerous in India, appear in the first instance.

*vṛścika* means poisonous spider and scorpion. In the following, since in the original text only the sharp bite is mentioned, consequently one had to consider the translation 'those snakes and spider-creatures with sharp bite that hide away in winter'. Nevertheless, to mention the scorpion (for the Indian word can also mean this) besides the snakes is possible. This leads to the translation: 'with the sharp bites *and sting*'.

47. The word *ratha* 'wagon', contrasted here with *anas* 'goods wagon', can also mean the chariot, but here in context is to be understood as the carriages of the lords for pleasure rides or travel purposes. So: 'where pleasure carriages roll, and goods vehicles drive'.

48. In the Indian language, *mṛga* 'wild' also means, as a noun, wild animals and relates to the more graceful animals of the forest, like deer, stag, gazelle, and so on. In this passage as an adjective 'wild' could also be related to the 'evil boar'. The meaning presumed here best suited to the actual thought of the whole verse comes out better when, instead of *sūkarāya* one reads *sūkareṇa.*

49. *Puruṣādas* 'who go for human beings' exactly corresponds, literally, to the man-eating tiger.

50. *Nachtmare und Schwarzalben,* 'nightmare and black dreams' is a free translation of the Indian *ārāyās* and *kimīdinas.*

51. The German *'Windsbraut'*, 'wind bride', approaches the Indian *mātariśvan* in so far as it, like the Indian word, connects the picture of the feminine aspect (*mātṛ* mother) with the storm-wind.

52. [No Notes]

53. After the 'danger zone' is completed with its rich description of the thunderstorm, there begins here the final section of the poem: 'The Earth and the human being', or 'The human being as lord of the Earth'.

54. The human being in Indian is *mānuṣa, manuṣya,* from the root *man* 'to think', which lies as the basis of the German

*'Mensch'* [as of the English 'man'], which is clearly related to the Indian word. The word *nāma* 'name' can be felt as an inversion of this root.[6] The phrase *aham asmi* 'I am' as the immediate beginning of the verse strongly emphasizes the human 'I', which we can feel too in the word *nāma*; the literal translation of the Indian would be: 'I am he who bears the name that he is the lord of the Earth,' and so on. For us there lies in this *nāma* the 'name, human being', which in the translation is consequently justified, even if the word *manuṣya* 'human being' as such is missing from this passage in the Indian.

55. [No Notes]

56. [No Notes]

57. *oṣadhi* (emphasis on the first syllable; *ṣ*, like 'sh') 'plant' includes herb and flower (the latter is not expressly mentioned in the original text).

58. The apparently fake, completely corrupt and questionable verse does not merit translation.

59. [No Notes]

60. 'The creative cosmic artist' is here the translation of the Indian name *Viśvakarman* (spoken Vishvakarman), the 'cosmic master-builder/ architect' and cosmic carpenter, according to Rudolf Steiner the Indian-Vedic name of the Christ.

Also, the name Aditi, here translated 'the human being's heavenly mother', the Indian Isis, mother of the gods.

The 'wish granter', Indian *kāmadhenu* or, as here, *kāmadughā*, actually: the cow that lets all wishes be milked, the 'wish-fulfilling cow'. In Egyptian, too, Isis is honoured as Earth and cow. (In Indian *one* word—*go*—signifies Earth and cow.)[7]

The 'high cosmic ordering' in Indian is *ṛta*, see the explanation to verse 1.

All further details concerning the deep background to this verse are in the Appendix.

61. [No Notes]

62. [No Notes]

63. The way in which the Earth is at the end addressed here as a 'wise seer' (*kave*, vocative of *kavi*) makes us think of Erda of Teutonic mythology. For the Vedic poet, the Earth is a spiritual entity who follows the course of world-events as a seeress.

# D. Appendix 1
# The Name of Christ and His Being in the Atharvaveda *Hymn*

## *1.*
## *Christ the Cosmic Truth*

It belongs to the unique and special characteristics of the Atharvaveda *Hymn* how here from an ancient time long before Christ certain wisdoms of the Earth and their connection with the cosmos reach us, which today can be felt as *Christ-Mysteries*, although the name 'Christ' belongs to a much later culture, to the Greek-Latin culture at the turning point of time. And even in the Veda we have met certain speech-sounds, which already in that ancient Indian Vedic time seems to carry sounds of the later Christ-name in a meaningful, significant way.

Immediately in the first verse, the beginning of the *Hymn*, we can feel touched by the world of Christ, where amongst the powers that spiritually carry the life of the Earth, in the first instance *satyaṃ bṛhat* 'the great truth of the world' is named. Here truth or truthfulness (*satyam*), is no longer an abstract concept, no longer something only theoretical, but a real spiritual power, which carries and guarantees the continuation of the Earth. As the mathematical, physical and technical rules, which are required to be applied, for example, in building a bridge, find the confirmation of their truth not only in abstract, theoretical thought-processes and calculations, but in the fact that the bridge built according to these rules is stable and does not collapse, that it proves to carry loads, in the same way for the Indian truth and truthfulness is proved not only through abstract 'proofs'—for purely theoretically one can prove everything, or many things, at the same time and also show the contrary—but through the way how that which human beings think and do is taken up or rejected by the world-events, how it proves to carry the loads of life. Novalis (*Fragmente*, ed. Kamnitzer, 308) expresses it in this sense: 'The difference between delusion and truth lies in the difference of their life-functions. Delusion lives off the truth; the truth contains its own life'; 'Untruth is the source of everything bad and evil' (306); 'All truth exists in its own inner harmony and concord' (292). In this sense, Christ also speaks in John's Gospel (3:21) of 'doing the truth' (*ποιῶν τὴν ἀλήθειαν*): 'But he who does what is true comes to the light, that it may be clearly seen that his deeds have been wrought in God.' Here the truth is something which one not only represents in thoughts or words, but it is a power carrying the world-events. The Greek word for truth (*a-letheia*) speaks of something that does not become lost in the dwindling of consciousness, but which can hold itself in the light of consciousness; the Indian word *satyam* speaks quite directly of that which is *essential being* (*sat*). In our sense, this essential being is that which in truth carries and orders the world-event, the *Christ-being*. Consequently, this Being, Christ, speaks of Himself by saying, 'I am the way, the truth and the life' (Jn. 14:6). The first word of the Indian *Hymn* relates to this essential Being, that which in truth carries and orders in the earthly sense world-events.

In Indian one speaks of *seven worlds*, of which the lowest is the sensory-visible earthly world (*bhūrloka*); the second is the 'transition world' (*bhuvarloka*); the third, the heavenly world of light (*svarloka*).

Then there follows: *maharloka* 'world of the higher light', *janaloka* 'world of the higher humanity', *tapaloka* 'world of the highest asceticism' (possibly: of the last trials or efforts). The seventh and highest world is *satyaloka* 'world of truth', in our sense the *world of Christ*.

## 2.
## *The Greek origin of the name 'Christ'; the speech sounds of the Indian kṛṣ, kṛṣṭi*

We feel especially close to the nearness of the Christ Earth-Mystery where we meet the word *kṛṣṭi*, which seems built of the sounds for the name Christ. It appears in three places in the *Hymn* (vv. 3, 4, 42) and means on the one hand 'ploughed field, seeded field', and on the other hand 'the human race, humanity'. One can become clearly aware how all these passages, at the same time—agriculture, seeded fields and humanity—speak about the 'seed of human beings'. One may recall here the early Gothic language where *manaseths*, actually *Menschensaat*, 'seed of human beings', is the word for 'humanity'. In v. 3 our translation seeks to do justice to the meaning of the Indian words through rendering: 'the Earth ... on which in the seed of the fields there grows nourishment for the seed of mankind' (the word *anna* 'nourishment' can also be found in all three passages).

Initially, one must be careful not to draw any far-reaching conclusions merely out of similar sounds between various languages. A certain unreliable, unscientific way of language research exists, of which in this direction much nonsense is perpetrated. Concerning the word *Χριστός* [*Kristos*], *Christ*, we know it stems in the first instance from the Greek language, deriving from the Greek *chriein* 'to anoint'; *chistos* is consequently 'the anointed one', the anointed King, and we will immediately recognize that it cannot concern any outer kingdom (Jn. 18:36) but that the inner kingdom, the kingdom in the 'I', is meant. It may be pointed out that also the Atharvaveda *Hymn* strongly emphasizes this 'kingdom in the "I"' in a way most surprising for the Indian situation, cf. v. 11 ('on it will stand, unconquerable, unsurpassed, uninjured, on this Earth, I', where in the Indian we have the same sequence of words, the same ending of the verse with *aham* 'I') and v. 53f., especially 54, 'Indeed, I, the human being, I am he ...' and so on, so that in v. 8 *rāṣṭre uttame* 'the epitome of true rulers' could be translated according to the meaning: 'to the highest rulership in the "I"'. If we want to pursue the connections and backgrounds of the *name* [strictly speaking, *title*] *Christ* also in the Atharvaveda, we can also add that meaning of the name Christ (out of the Greek as the original) resounds in the *Hymn to the Earth* in various places. Consequently, in this consideration of ours there can be no question of having disregarded this meaning of the name of Christ, which for the scholars is alone relevant.

But as clearly correct as this derivation of the name Christ out of the Greek language is, so sure is the other consideration that the initiates, who in the fourth post-Atlantean cultural epoch gave this name, during their name-giving had further contexts in mind than only the one derivation from the Greek *chriein*, 'to anoint'. For those creating language, fashioning the word in accordance with its spiritual content, not only does the academic derivation, the historical etymology of the word, come into consideration but that which is directly revealed in the structure of the sounds of a word still stimulated by the inherent primordial qualities. It would be meaningless to employ such a sensing of the primordial qualities with regard to words used in everyday contexts, to words that are secondhand, but this application of the perspective of the archetypal word is justified with regard to the name of the divinity and especially the name Christ, of which the Bible declares that in Himself He bears all the creative Mysteries of the cosmic Word (John 1:1-5). Here alongside the outer etymology, whose justification is never denied, it is also justified with the interpretation of the name to draw on that experience of the sounds which still draws directly on the archetypal nature of every single sound of speech.[8] In this sense Novalis distinguishes a double etymology, which he termed the *genetic* and the *pragmatic* (whereby he appears to understand under 'pragmatic' the academic, historical etymology). And we may be sure that the initiates who in a specific cultural epoch give such names, which also in the Greco-Latin cultural epoch found the *name Christ*, with this name-giving proceeded not only from the one-sided academic etymology but also from that other, higher etymology, the primordial meaning of the sounds.

Were we once to ask such an initiate, who in modern times has penetrated in the deepest way into the Christ-Earth-Mysteries, then we ask Jakob Boehme how he understands the name Christ, out of the primordial element of the word and language and out of the sounds. We find in the book *De Signatura Rerum*, Chapter 7, 31,[9] the following—whereby Boehme, who is so closely connected to nature, and out of all the phenomena of nature, 'out of all the chalices of the flowers', one would like to say, perceiving the Mysteries of the world, used the word '*Natursprache*', the 'natural language', completely in the sense of that which we here called the 'primal language element of speech', the primordial element in the sounds of speech:

> *Christ, that means in the language of nature, someone who breaks through,* to take the power from wrath, a gleam of light in the darkness; a transmutation, since the desire for love rules over the desire for fire, in the same way as over wrath the light rules over the darkness.[10]

Here, 'Christ' from the understanding of the sounds means for the initiate 'the One who breaks through' or 'the One who penetrates through', the One breaking or penetrating through death, or darkness, who wrestles life from death and light from the darkness, *Who penetrates Earth itself* with His life and with His light. It may be recalled how in the symbol of the cross—a Russian *krest,* obviously related to *Christos*—these connections are expressed.

Such connections are also not foreign to the Indian culture. In the Indian trinity Brahma—Vishnu—Shiva, Vishnu is the Son-god, who in various earthly forms goes through various earthly incarnations (*avatāra*s), in order to incarnate as a human being in Krishna. (Rudolf Steiner has pointed out that we are to see in Krishna an early, a '*māyā*-incarnation', of that being who, before had remained in spiritual worlds and then in the [Nathan] Jesus-child of Luke's Gospel had experienced his first real incarnation. This name of the Indian 'Son-god' Vishnu is derived from a root *viś* (spoken vish), which means 'break in, penetrate'. The Indian Son-god Vishnu receives his name because in three great (symbolic) steps (often mentioned in the Veda) he has penetrated the Earth—the third and last of these steps led him again beyond the earthly world, leading him upwards into the world of highest light. But also, in the Atharvaveda which is full of Mysteries of Christ, Vishnu, the Son-god, appears as the one traversing and penetrating the Earth in v. 10 of the *Hymn to the Earth*:

> She who once measured out the divine duality of the Morning Star,
> who was traversed by Vishnu, the all-penetrating one,
> ... she, our Earth, ...

All this leads the discussion once again to the Mysteries of the pure sounds of the name 'Christ' sounding so uniquely out of the word *krishti, kṛṣṭi,* appearing in several places in the Atharvaveda *Hymn,* meaning not only ploughed field, seeded field, but also the human race, mankind. It would not be correct, we said, to draw in a fantastic manner far-reaching conclusions out of mere arbitrary coincidences. But here the situation is quite different, where it concerns the Mysteries of the name of Christ and the quite conscious name-giving by initiates (Christian as well as Indian) drawing on the primordial language. Here, linking to that which Jakob Boehme's explanation of the name of Christ (Christ as the one who breaks through or penetrates) and what has been said of the meaning of the Indian name for Christ, Vishnu ('the One who breaks through, penetrates'), it points to the actual meaning and primordial derivation of the Indian word *kṛṣṭi* (seeded field and mankind). It comes from a root *kṛṣ* (spoken krish), 'pull through, break through, furrow, penetrate, overcome', initially from the plough being pulled through the furrow, but then also used in a higher, spiritual sense. Thus, the picture of drawing the plough through the Earth, the drawing of the furrow with the plough stands in the Indian word *kṛṣṭi,* appearing three times in the *Hymn to the Earth.* And when we regard the unique double meaning of the word (which calls before the soul the Gothic *manaseths,* mankind, actually 'seed of humanity'), then we feel in a unique manner in touch with the Christ-Mysteries of the Earth, which the Atharvaveda *Hymn* completely fulfils. The pictures in John's Gospel (12:24) appear before the soul, of Christ as the grain of wheat or seed that is sunk into the Earth, that dying taken up into the Earth brings forth much fruit. Thereby, moreover, the whole context that exists between Christ and the Earth, Christ and mankind, mankind and the Earth in general, contexts which we can characterize in the sense of Christian recognition as the *Mysteries of bread*, Mysteries that were already felt in the Eleusinian Mysteries of the Greeks and there found a significant expression [also appear before the soul]. Moreover, in the Atharvaveda *Hymn* the 'Lord of the bread'[11] (verse 40, Indian *Bhaga*; we find shortly before v. 42, in which the Mysteries of *kṛṣṭi* are heard once more) recalls these contexts. And it can be felt as really significant when in v. 3 alongside this 'Mystery of the bread' there is also heard the 'Mystery of the cup' (which then in v. 60 once again finds direct and profound expression); then the *pūrvapeye dadhātu* at the end of the verse 3, which we have translated as 'may it allow us to drink from its untouched freshness', means quite literally, 'may she (the Earth) *admit us to the first drink* (out of her cup or chalice)'.

Finally, it should be pointed out, how in the word *kṛṣṭi* (meaning 'seeded field' and 'mankind', reminding us of the sounds of the name of Christ) there lies the root *kṛṣ*, which is also the root of the name Krishna (*Kṛṣṇa*), thus allowing this name to participate in all the contexts of Christ that arise from it. As the adjective *kṛṣṇa* means 'black' (to be found with this meaning in v. 11 of the *Hymn*: 'on the brown, *black*, reddish, many-coloured earthly ground ...'), it is probably correct to think of the black colour of the earth in the furrow loosened by the plough. So little as it would be justified to derive the word 'Christ' in the sense of an historic etymology directly from the Indian Krishna or thereby to wish to connect them (all attempts in this direction here and there have to be dismissed as unscientific), yet on the other side, it is nevertheless true, that the contexts of the name 'Christ' with the higher primordial speech indicated by Boehme, rediscovered in the Indian *kṛṣ, kṛṣṭi,* at the same time also encompass Krishna, the name of the Indian saviour.

## 3.
## *The name 'Christ' and the speech from the heart of the Earth*

To the verses of the Indian *Hymn* which are completely filled by the Christ–Earth Mysteries, to which especially belongs v. 8, where it speaks of the beginning of creation and in connection with these creation Mysteries of the Earth, of the 'divine heart of the Earth in the highest heaven': 'she, whose heart, the Earth's undying heart, is in the highest heaven, enveloped by cosmic truth.' That the word *satya* (truth, truthfulness) here translated as 'cosmic truth' signifies the world of Christ, has already been mentioned. The outer, astronomical-cosmogonic observation shows us how with the creation of the planets we have to regard the Sun as the actual centre, the heart of the whole system. And this initially more outer view is deepened through anthroposophy towards the spiritual view. It is shown how life on the Earth originally connected with the life of the Sun. The spiritual of the Earth related to the spiritual aspect of the Sun, then the Earth becomes the decisive place of the development of destiny of humanity (carrying in itself the meaning of the whole). It becomes the stage of history, but with the separation of Earth and Sun the actual living centre for all human existence, for all human development was to have remained in the etheric realm of the Sun. Through the Fall of humanity this original connection with the life of the Sun has become estranged. (Further details in Rudolf Steiner, *Karmic Relationships*, Vol. 3 [GA 237].) The *Christ-event*, of the Mystery of Golgotha, means that in it the spiritual Sun-life has connected with the Earth, that it has penetrated the Earth anew, so that the Earth again becomes a seed of a new cosmic, a new Sun-life. The heart of the Earth, which has remained in the cosmic, the 'highest heaven' as the Indian says, has remained in the Sun-life. In the Christ-deed of Golgotha it has, as it were, become connected to the Earth and humanity,[12] and in the human heart it has begun to beat again in the Earth, in the human heart that opens up to the deed of Christ.

Quite extraordinary depths open up at that place in the Atharvaveda *Hymn* where it speaks of the 'heart, the immortal heart of the Earth, in the highest heaven'. Originally the heart in the Sun-life included all earthly life; the Sun-life again had its heart in the highest starry life, of which it is a part: as earthly life is woven into the context of the Sun, so the spiritual Sun-life is woven into the starry context. These contexts again, which we today dimly divine as *Christ-contexts*, are the actual Christ-Earth-Mysteries.

In the Atharvaveda the heart of the Earth is otherwise mentioned (v. 35, 'I will not, you pure one, hit into the marrow of your life, I will not bore through your heart.') and of the gold in the heart of the Earth (in the 'breasts of the Earth', as the Atharvaveda says, vv. 6, 26, see also v. 44). Spiritual science tells us that earthly gold expresses physically the Sun-gold, the sunlight in the heart of the Earth (in the same way as iron corresponds with the planetary element of Mars, and other metals to the essence of other planets). The 'Zarathustra' saying of

Friedrich Nietzsche, 'The heart of the Earth is gold' [*Thus Spoke Zarathustra*, 40, Great Events], consequently closely leads us, touched on in the Atharvaveda, to the Mysteries of the heart of the Earth in the highest heaven, of the context of earthly life with the sunlight and starry life. Furthermore, we recall how amongst the human inner organs, as spiritual science teaches, that also correspond to the planets; the heart corresponds to the Sun (as the liver corresponds to Jupiter, the gall to Mars, the kidney to Venus, and so on).

*The heart is truly the Sun within the human being.* Within this, too, deep Christ-Mysteries lie, which resound in the Atharvaveda. In Indian Yoga writings we read what is revealed in supersensory vision of the brightly radiant lotus-flower in the human heart with eight petals, in the midst of which is a radiant Sun-circle. (Justinus Kerner, *Seherin von Prevorst*, describes similar visions.) This Sun-like 'flower of the heart', is for the Yoga practitioner the organ of higher knowledge. For all head knowledge, all mere intellectual knowledge is for the Indian but world-delusion, *māyā*. For him the heart is the truthful, the alone truly knowing centre in the human being. We also recall the presentation in the Egyptian Book of the Dead, where the soul of the dead appears before Osiris and is placed there before a world-judgement scale. In the one pan the heart is laid of the one who has died, and in the other the 'feather of truthfulness' is laid, and only if the scale is to be found in balance can the person who has died experience the world of light of Osiris. In this sense, the Atharvaveda also says [v. 8] that the immortal heart of the Earth in the highest heaven, 'is enveloped by cosmic truth' (*satyena āvṛtam*). In this is expressed the spiritual connection of the heart with the highest of all worlds, the Christ-world.

Having summarized everything here, we may, this time from another side, once more approach the primordial word-Mystery of the name of Christ. With this aspect of the 'primordial language' or 'primordial word', it is not as with academic etymology that only one derivation is jutifiable, the only possible one. But, from various sides, the approach is revealed to the actual Mystery of the word, or the name can only be found within. After we have placed here all the connections of the heart of the Earth in the highest heaven, of the heart and Earth, heart and Sun, Sun and Earth, Sun and gold, heart and gold,[13] we want finally to focus on the Indian word for 'heart', *hṛdaya* (emphasis on the first syllable, formed through the vowel *ṛ*, spoken 'hrídaya'), as it appears in vv. 8 and 35, which is only a continuation of the simple root *hṛd*. This *hṛd* heart—also in the conventional academic etymology—in its sounds is the same as the Germ. *'Herz'*, Eng. 'heart'. In the Greek *καρδία* kardia means 'heart'. It appears in the gospel where (Matt. 12:40) it is mentioned that Christ will stay for three days and nights 'in the heart of the Earth' (as all the versions translate). Comparing the Indian *hṛd* with the Gk. *kard* ... helps us to recognize or presume that the original initial sound of the primordial word lies between h and k, that it must have been a sound similar to ch (as the Indian h, for example, in the word *brahman*, in general often has something of Germ. ch [cf. ch in Eng. 'loch']). Thus, for *Herz*, heart, we have an archetypal form *chṛd*, which from another side has a touch of the primordial name of the Christ-name and seems to speak directly of the Christ-Mysteries of the human heart, and the 'heart of the Earth', revealing to us, as it were, Christ's Being as the actual key to all the Mysteries of the heart.

## 4.
## *The Earth-Star Mystery of the word* Kristall, *'crystal', in Indian and Egyptian*

We cannot conclude the observations on the Christ-Earth-connections in the Atharvaveda *Hymn to the Earth* without considering those most significant of all verses to do with Christ, in which also the chalice Mystery of the Earth is mentioned. It is v. 60 where the Indian poet, similar to v. 24, where the Mystery of the scent of the Earth is mentioned in connection with the essential scent prepared by the gods for the wedding feast of the Sun-goddess that once more allows us to see deeply into the Mysteries of creation, into primordial creation contexts of the Earth. The World Creator is mentioned here by two names. The one is the name Prajāpati (spoken 'Pradshāpati', emphasis on the third to last syllable), the 'first-born of the high world-order'; that means here, as everywhere in the Indian culture, the creator-god is not the father, who is here equal with the sacred world-order, the *ṛtạ*, but the Son-god, the first-born and only-born of the father, who in the primordial, original creation at first appears to the light of day 'swimming on a lotus-leaf'.

And then, above all, this being of the creative Son-god appears directly at the beginning of the verse with that name of which Rudolf Steiner has always said (see *The East in the Light of the West*, GA 113, lect. 6, Munich, 28 Aug. 1909) that it is the Indian Vedic name of the Christ-being, with the name Vishvakarman (*Viśvakarman*), literally the 'All-Creator / Creator of All'. It is this Vishvakarman, to whom two songs are dedicated (X, 81 & 82) of the Indian Rigveda, of whom the old seers, the Rishis, emphasized that he still lies 'above their sphere'. He is regarded by the

Indians, especially as the *heavenly carpenter*, the 'master builder / architect of the world', as we can also say with the beautiful expression of Christian Morgenstern.[14] The *artistic point of view* of the world-creative [impulse] finds special expression in this Indian name, Vishvakarman. For this reason—initially foreign for the Western reader—was the name in our translation rendered as 'the divine, creative World-Artist'. The second part of the name contains the Indian word *karman* which, derived from *kṛ*, 'to do, make, establish', depicts in the well-known concept of destiny, *karma*, human destiny as that which is self-fashioned, self-established, as the human being's own creative deed, related to the Lat. *creare* ('to create').

It can be recognized as something lying in the direction of the Christ-Earth-Mystery, how here already in the Atharvaveda the [tremendous] sacrifice is mentioned in which that creative Christ-Vishvakarman Being connected Itself with the Earth in certain primordial conditions of its becoming (where it, still hidden in higher elements, was only slowly to come into appearance as the physical Earth). In anthroposophy, too (see the lecture-cycle *Christ and the Spiritual World*, GA 149, Leipzig 1913), it is mentioned, how not only in the event of Golgotha (where Christ's Incarnation entered [completely] into the physical) but already on earlier levels of development, a penetration of the earthly element on the part of the Christ-Being took place, but taking place in higher elements.[15] In connection with the Mysteries of creation of the Vishvakarman-Christ Being, the Atharvaveda *Hymn* touches in this verse the Mystery of the Earth in a deeply meaningful way as a chalice-Mystery: 'You (Earth) are the chalice vessel', which, as Earth, was still hidden to earthly senses, as it were, in hiding, enclosed in a protecting sheath. With this

Christ-connection, it is very significant how the Earth here is celebrated as a spiritual being, as 'the heavenly mother of human beings'. The Indian name appearing here in the original text is *aditi*. It is derived by the Indians from *a-dita* 'unbound', *a-diti* 'unboundness' and understood as primal eternity, infinity, before the beginning of all things. But we may recall that in the Egyptian language[16] *adit* is also one of the names of Isis. *Aditi*, the Indian mother of the gods, venerated as such in the Rigveda, is the Indian form of the Egyptian Isis. Like Isis she is the heavenly comforter and advocate of human beings, the Indian-Egyptian Madonna, the same being who then becomes the centre of the Christian veneration of Mary. And we know how intimately the Mystery of Mary is connected to the chalice of the Last Supper. The heavenly soma drink, which as the epitome of the highest cosmic essence is enjoyed by Indra (in v. 38 of the Atharvaveda *Hymn* the soma drink prepared for Indra is mentioned), is in the Rigveda (VIII, 48, 2) brought into immediate relationship to Aditi. As it is said concerning the Egyptian Naith-Isis, so it is also said of the Indian Aditi-Isis that she is everything that was and will be (Rigveda I, 89, 10: *Aditir yātam Aditir yanitvam*), whereby quite directly even the first verse of the Atharvaveda *Hymn* it is heard that she is the governess of everything 'that was and is to come' (if we translate literally). Like the divine mother Aditi in the Atharvaveda *Hymn* v. 60, so too in the Egyptian culture Isis appears as the *Earth*. This means that descending from her original revelation in the stars and the Moon, Isis, after the onslaught from Typhon-Ahriman, finally reveals herself during a certain stage of earthly development as the *Earth*, and as a symbol of the Earth she is adorned with the horns of the cow, she finally appears as a cow. This again is important for the Indian connections where *one* word, *go* (related to the Gk. *ge*, Gäa), means 'earth' and 'cow'.[17] Moreover, in vv. 60/61, the Mystery completely connected to the Earth, of the heavenly mother Aditi (who is addressed as the Earth), appears at the same time as the Mystery of the cow, for the Indian word *kāmadughā* (otherwise *kāmadhenu*), freely translated as the one granting wishes, is the 'wish-fulfilling cow' famous in Indian mythology, the cow from which one can milk any wish. At every turn the Atharvaveda *Hymn* shows itself through and through penetrated by the *cow motif*, so common in the whole Indian Veda, especially the Rigveda. In the same way as in the Egyptian culture, the Mystery of the Earth is also everywhere connected in the Indian culture with the cow, which especially in the Atharvaveda plays a great role. There it is also mentioned how cosmic Mysteries, indeed stellar Mysteries are mirrored in the bovine organism.[18] In the Indian Aditi-Earth, as in the Egyptian Isis, as we can also say, the starry Mysteries meet the earthly Mysteries. This is perhaps also the hidden meaning of that marriage, mentioned in verse 24 of the *Hymn*.

## *Conclusion*

After all this, we return to the hidden riddle of the name of Christ and its expression in the Indian [language]. In verses 60-61, the way the Mystery of creation of Vishvakarman-Christ is connected with the Mystery of the Earth and the Mystery of the chalice of Aditi-Isis—a starry chalice-Mystery, which then becomes that of the chalice of the Moon, of the chalice of the plant blossoms, ultimately of the chalice-Mystery of the earthly, physical body, Gk. *soma*[19]—once more causes certain connections of the Christ-name with the primordial language to appear, developed in more detail in the essay 'On the name Isis' in *From the Mysteries* [TL 2020]. There it concerns that key of the primordial name of 'Christ' contained in the German [and English] word '*Kristall*', 'crystal', thought by scholars to derive from the Gk. *kryros* 'frost', pointing initially to the ice-crystal of the snowflake.

But the ice-crystal of the snowflake is once again a symbol of comprehensive cosmic Mysteries, which then also speak to us (beyond all 'etymology') in the primordial speech in the words '*Kristall*' (crystal) and '*Kristus*' (*Christus*, Christ). The wonderful starry forms of the formed ice-crystal of the snowflake, tell us, as it were, how all earthly matter, which in the snow has its first, purest, virginal expression, condensed out of its cosmic essence of starry, primordial light. In the Egyptian primordial name Isis itself (*Ist*, *Iset*, *Isis*, that have emerged out of the purely consonantal *H-S-T*), these creative Mysteries can be seen and felt purely out of the sounds (more details in the above-mentioned essay, 'On the name Isis'). These are those Mysteries of Isis, towards which the name of the divine mother Aditi, as it appears in the Vishvarkarman-Christ verse of the Atharvaveda *Hymn*, contains the indication.

Furthermore, it could then be shown, how the Egyptian name Isis (*I-s-t*) is contained in both the words *Kristall*, crystal, and in the name Christ (*Kristus*) connected to that primordial root *kṛ*, which in Indian means 'to do, make, fashion', and etymologically corresponds with the Lat. *creare*, 'to create'. In this sense the 'crystal' reveals to us deepest Mysteries, the Isis-cosmic-Mysteries of the Christ (*Kristus*) the Creator. Christ appears here as the One Who reveals out of the forces of the primordial light, of the primordial starry light, and of the primordial starry essence (for which the ice-crystal of the snowflake is the earthly symbol) fashioning in the earthly material essence. Out of cosmic, starry-light-essence, He reveals the Mystery of the cosmic starry light weaving the miracle of the earthly essence in the earthly material. In the mountain crystal, we behold how cosmic form and cosmic light still shine through in the earthly material structure of the stone. The word *Kristall* speaks to us, how the Mystery of the stone relates to that of the stars. And the allusion in the name 'Christ' shows us again this stone-star-Mystery as a cosmic-Christ-Mystery; it speaks to us of the revelation of the *Kristus in Weltall*, Christ in the Universe (*Krist-all*).[20]

The creative Christ-Earth-Mystery connects with the Starry-Earth-Mystery of the mother of matter, Isis, in the word 'crystal'. The Mystery of the name Christ (*Kristus*) experiences through this a new revelation out of the cosmic element, which meaningfully links with the two other interpretations of the name 'Christ' out of the primordial language, already given above. And as we found for the two other interpretations of the name 'Christ' the starting point in the content and in the words of the Atharvaveda *Hymn*, for this third interpretation, too, a connection could be found in those verses 60/61, which so meaningfully connect the Mystery of the chalice of the starry mother and Earth-mother, Aditi-Isis, with the Mystery of the world-creator, Vishvakarman-Christ.

# E. Appendix 2

## 1.

## *The Indian Hymn of Creation of the Rigveda (X, 129)* *(The German translation of Hermann Beckh put into English)*

1. There was not—then, before all time—a state of being, and also no state of non-being,
As yet there was no realm of air and no sky beyond.
What was it, then, which this whole world still kept hidden?
Where was the unfathomable deep lap of water?

2. As yet there was no death, no life freed from death.
As yet no difference between day and night.
A wafting breath without a wind, caused only by the primordial power of its own being,
Thus was the divine primordial One, besides Whom there was no other.

3. Only darkness, hiding still in the primordial lap of denser darkness, prevailed there in the primordial beginning.
Undifferentiated, the whole universe was primordial waves.
That which, enveloped by the emptiness of the cosmos, was there as the seed of becoming
Came by itself to unfold through the power of spiritual deepening which, brooding, awakening cosmic warmth.

4. The primordial want of cosmic longing started to become, there in the primordial beginning;
This longing was the first creative shoot of World Thinking.
The thread, linking over from non-being to the revelation of existence, wise seers, seeking with their visionary power, found in the depths of human hearts.

5. Crossing wide spaces, the light-ray of their spirit-eye reached out.
Did an above and a below already exist?
There were only spirit-forces, beings able to fructify,
And others who receiving, grew into the widths.
Below there was maternal primordial power, above the fructifying spirit-working beam.

6. How the unity of all-being there becomes the multitude of today,
Who in truth would know this, be able to proclaim it to us?
The gods themselves came later into being *through* this becoming.
Whence it all came, who of them would know to proclaim it to us?

7. How everything branched into multiplicity, whence all this becoming took its origin,
And if it was at all a creative working,
He, Who in the highest heaven beholds everything,
Only He alone may knowingly proclaim it to us,
In so far as even His knowledge—is silence.

## 2.

## *The beginning of Genesis (the biblical Story of Creation) (The German translation of Hermann Beckh put into English)*

In the spirit-thought of the primordial beginnings, the creative beings, the Elohim, wove heaven and earth.

And the earth was a pulsing being in becoming and darkness reigned over the depths of the world.

And the spirit of the Godhead wafting in the sacred wind was brooding over the primordial water[s].

Then the divine cosmic Word spoke, Let there be Light! And there was Light.

And the Godhead of the Elohim beheld the glory of the Light.

Then the creative divine Thought divided light and darkness.

The light He called day and the darkness night.

Thus the evening and then the morning of the world was *one* day [Heb. 'Day One].

## 3.

## *Christian Morgenstern 'Die Weidenkätzchen'*

*Kätzchen ihr der Weide, / wie aus grauer Seide,*
*wie aus grauem Samt! / O ihr Silberkätzchen,*
*Sagt mir doch ihr Schätzchen, / sagt, woher ihr stammt.*
*«Wollens gern dir sagen: / Wir sind ausgeschlagen*
*aus dem Weidenbaum, / haben winterüber*
*drin geschlafen, Lieber, / in tieftiefem Traum!»*
*In dem dürren Baume / in tieftiefem Traume*

*habt geschlafen ihr? / In dem Holz, dem harten,*
*war, ihr weichen, zarten, / euer Nachtquartier?*
*«Musst dich recht besinnen: / Was da träumte drinnen,*
*waren wir noch nicht, / wie wir jetzt im Kleide*
*blühn von Samt und Seide / hell im Sonnenlicht.*
*Nur all wie Gedanken / lagen wir im schlanken*
*grauen Baumgeäst; / unsichtbare Geister,*
*die der Weltbaumeister / dort verweilen lässt.»*
*Kätzchen ihr der Weide, / wie aus grauer Seide,*
*wie aus grauem Samt! O ihr Silberkätzchen,*
*ja, nun weiss, ihr Schätzchen, / ich, woher ihr stammt.*

['Pussy Willows' (prose tr.)

Pussies of the willow like grey silk, like grey velvet! O, you silver kittens, tell me, you darlings, tell me from where you come.

'We are happy to tell you: we burst out of the willow tree, have throughout the winter slept within, my dear, in deep, deep dream.'

In the arid tree, in deep, deep dream did you sleep? In the wood, the hard wood, you delicate creatures, was your night quarters?

'You have to remember: what was inside, dreaming, was not yet we as we now bloom in dresses of velvet and silk, bright in the sunlight.

Only like thoughts we lay in the slim, grey branches of the tree; as invisible spirits, which the Master-Builder of the World causes to tarry.'

Pussies of the willow, like grey silk, like grey velvet! O, you silver kittens, now I know, you darlings, from where you come.]

# Notes

1. These are:
   1. the *Rigveda* (Ṛgveda, *ṛ* is the vowel variant of r), the Veda of sacrificial hymns to the gods;
   2. the *Sāmaveda*, musical supplement of the preceding;
   3. the *Yajurveda* (spoken Yadshurveda), the Veda of the sacrificial verses, which in the extensive Brahmana literature (the word Brāhmaṇa—has h somewhat audible—the emphasis on the first syllable) with its mystical-explanatory presentation of the ceremonial rituals of the Indians contains additions;
   4. the *Atharvaveda*, the Veda of the magical verses and discussions, with interspersed longer Hymns to divine beings, of which the *Hymn to the Earth* is an outstanding example.

   This fourth Veda is not part of the canon of the orthodox brahmins. For us today it is in many respects the most interesting and in part the most beautiful.
2. Here, also in the anthroposophical sense, a prehistorical age is meant, which is determined by the spring equinox in the zodiac-sign of the Twins, that is, it reaches back to the sixth millennium BCE. As in the primordial Indian age of the Veda, the much younger Avesta contains only a late echo of this primal Persian age. More on this can be found in the author's *Zarathustra* (in *From the Mysteries*, TL 2020).
3. The language is Old Vedic Sanskrit with its partly still problematic meanings of words, because it originated during an earlier phase of human consciousness. The meanings are not always as straightforwardly established as those of a modern language or even of later classical Sanskrit.
4. The Arabic numerals relate to the numbering of the verses comprising the original text (three verses have been omitted in the translation as presumably non-genuine); the Roman numbers supplied by the translator mark the sub-sections.
5. Cf. H. Brugsch, *Religion und Mythologie der alten Ägypter*, Leipzig 1891, p. 343f., 656.
6. Cf. the writer's book on *John's Gospel*, Part A, Chapter 7.

7. Speech / the Word (vāc) is also 'cow'—*Ed.*
8. More details in the author's lectures 'Etymology and the Meaning of Speech-Sounds', 'The Physical and the Spiritual Origin of Speech' and '"Let there be Light": The Biblical Primal Words of Creation' in *The Source of Speech*, TL 2019, 112-180.
9. Jakob Boehme, Germ. original 7, 31. Online tr. The Signature of All Things, 7, 29: translated by John Ellistone 1651, revised for the 1781 'William Law Edition': The Works of Jacob Behmen, Volume IV http://jacobboehmeonline.com/yahoo_site_admin/assets/docs/signature.198144740.pdf/
10. Werke. Deutscher Klassiker Verlag im Taschenbuch Band 33. Frankfurt am Main. 2009, p. 584. Tr. A.S.
11. This is a very imaginative interpretation that, one feels, could have been explained a bit more. 'Bread' as such plays no role in the Vedic imagination whatsoever. *Bhaga* means 'wealth, prosperity' and so on—*Ed.*
12. For an exact rendering of the anthroposophical knowledge, there also belongs that with this connection the highest kernel (*ātman*) of Christ's being has remained within the life of the Sun.
13. Homeopathic medicine uses finely potentized gold as a remedy for heart conditions.
14. Cf. the charming, profound poem '*Die Weidenkätzchen*' ['Pussy Willows'] from the children's book *Klein Irmchen*, which we reproduce in the Appendix since it is too little known.
15. This sacrifice, also referred to as the 'pre-earthly deeds of Christ' (see also lecture, Pforzheim 7 March 1914), summarizes three sacrifices involving the Nathan-being at three critical periods of earthly human evolution to preserve the objectivity of the senses, to secure order in the life-body and to establish a measure of harmony in the astral body—*Tr.*
16. See Brugsch, *Religion und Mythologie der alten Ägypter*, Leipzig 1891, p. 306.
17. This is not the only Indian word for 'Earth', usually—even in the Atharvaveda—*pṛthivī* or *bhūmi* also means Earth.
18. In *Karmic Relationships*, Vol. 1 [GA 235], Rudolf Steiner speaks of the connection between the earthly Mysteries, as they were known to the most ancient primitive races, with the Mysteries of the cow. He mentions that there are immediate cosmic, star-Mysteries and cosmic rhythms, which are revealed in the organism and in the

life-functions of the cow. Undoubtedly, the great role the cow plays in the Rigveda, as in all the Vedic writings, has a great deal to do with these Mysteries. More is involved than the mere indication, assumed by the scholars, of the simple agricultural connections in which these early primitive people still lived. These deeper Earth-cow-Mysteries are completely evident in the Atharvaveda, hidden behind everything that is said about the cow as the provider of milk. This already appears in the *Hymn to the Earth.* And above all there is a hymn devoted to the cow, Atharvaveda X 10, that directly relates the things mentioned in anthroposophy. At the end of this *Hymn* (v. 33) it is plainly said how in the cosmic rhythm, the cosmic-star-rhythm (*ṛta*) that is reflected in the earthly experience, the cow is inserted (*ṛtaṃ hy asyām arpitam*). What Rudolf Steiner describes concerning the cow is thus also directly confirmed out of Indian sources.

19. The word in Indian means the juice of the soma plant, also the soma of the stars, moreover, also the Moon.
20. Cf. 'Christ in the Universe', Alice Meynell (1847-1922), reprinted (for example) in *The Oxford Book of English Verse.* Ed. Nicholson & Lee. Oxford: The Clarendon Press 1917. Also, readily available online—*Tr.*